Harriet Tubman

History Maker Bios

Maryann N. Weidt

L LERNER PUBLICATIONS COMPANY • MINNEAPOLIS

To Pearl Belton
(and the Visible Woman)

Illustrations by Tim Parlin

Text copyright © 2003 by Maryann N. Weidt
Illustrations copyright © 2003 by Lerner Publications Company

Lerner Publications Company
A division of Lerner Publishing Group
241 First Avenue North
Minneapolis, MN 55401 U.S.A.

Website address: www.lernerbooks.com

Library of Congress Cataloging-in-Publication Data

Weidt, Maryann N.
      Harriet Tubman / by Maryann N. Weidt.
         p.   cm. — (History maker bios)
      Includes bibliographical references (p.) and index.
      ISBN: 0–8225–4676–0 (lib. bdg. : alk. paper)
      1. Tubman, Harriet, 1820?–1913—Juvenile literature. 2. Slaves—United
   States—Biography—Juvenile literature. 3. African American women—
   Biography—Juvenile literature. 4. Underground railroad—Juvenile literature.
   5. Antislavery movements—United States—History—19th century—Juvenile
   literature. [1. Tubman, Harriet, 1820?–1913. 2. Slaves. 3. African Americans—
   Biography. 4. Women—Biography. 5. Underground railroad.] I. Title. II. Series.
   E444.T82 W45 2003
   973.7'115—dc21   2002005527

Manufactured in the United States of America
1 2 3 4 5 6 – JR – 08 07 06 05 04 03

TABLE OF CONTENTS

A Price On Her Head

INTRODUCTION

Harriet Tubman worked on the Underground Railroad. This railroad had nothing to do with trains. It was a group of people like Harriet who helped slaves escape to freedom in the North in the 1800s.

Before Harriet saved other slaves, she was a slave herself. Even as a little girl, she worked very hard and was beaten often. In 1849, she escaped to Philadelphia, where slavery was illegal. Her angry master and people who wanted a reward searched for her. Still, Harriet made nineteen trips back into the dangerous South and rescued over three hundred slaves. She became famous as a person who was not afraid to risk her life to help others.

This is her story.

1 BORN INTO SLAVERY

By the time Harriet Ross was six years old, she knew all about hard work. She worked all day, almost every day, on a farm near Bucktown, Maryland. Harriet's mother and father were slaves. And right from the moment Harriet was born, in about 1820, she was a slave, too. So were her ten brothers and sisters. A white man owned them all.

One of the jobs Harriet had to do was check muskrat traps. She waded into an icy river to see if any animals had been caught. Her feet were bare and her shirt was thin. Once, when Harriet caught a fever from doing this cold, wet job, her master became angry. He thought she was faking her illness so she wouldn't have to work.

Soon, red spots appeared on her body. She had the measles. But the master wouldn't let Harriet's mother take care of her. Harriet's mother had to work in the fields, with the other slaves.

Most slaves had little free time for playing or relaxing. Even young children had to work almost every day.

Harriet lay alone on the floor of her family's one-room shack. She thought about the master's children. When they got sick, they stayed in a warm bed in a big house. Harriet wondered why her family had to live this way.

Harriet recovered from the measles, and she grew up strong. By the time she was ten years old, she worked in the fields with the adult slaves. She harvested wheat and husked corn. She drove an ox cart and plow. Sometimes she helped her father cut wood and haul logs. Everyone said she worked as hard as any man. In one day, she could cut a pile of wood four feet high.

Many planters, like the man who owned Harriet, lived in big, fancy houses.

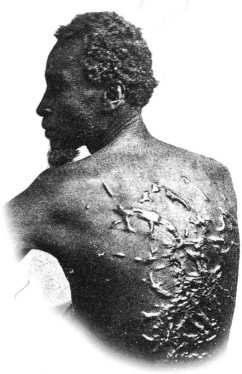

This slave's back was scarred from whippings.

Harriet worked from sunrise to sunset. A man called an overseer watched the slaves' every move, and he was cruel. He whipped the slaves if he thought they weren't working hard enough. Harriet's back was slashed with scars from the whip.

Sometimes, stories about a different kind of life in the North were whispered among the slaves. Harriet listened carefully. It was against the law to own slaves there. Black people were free. At night, Harriet dreamed about being free.

A master and his overseer (on horseback)

When Harriet was about fifteen, a slave named Jim sneaked away from the fields. The overseer noticed and chased after him with his whip. Harriet followed them both.

The overseer caught up to Jim at a store in town and began yelling at him. Jim bolted out the door and ran. The overseer ordered Harriet to stop him. Instead, Harriet stood in the door and blocked the overseer's path. The overseer was furious. He picked up a two-pound iron weight and threw it at Harriet. It struck her on the forehead, and she collapsed onto the floor, bleeding. Everyone thought she was dead.

Harriet wasn't dead, but she was barely alive. All that winter, she lay on the floor of her family's tiny shack. Her mother took care of her when she could. Other slaves looked in on her and wondered if she would survive. The overseer tried to sell her, but no one wanted a half-dead slave.

NOT SO SWEET

One day when Harriet was about seven years old, she noticed a bowl of sugar lumps on her master's kitchen table. Harriet had never tasted anything sweet. When she thought nobody was looking, she snatched one. But the master's wife caught her. To avoid a whipping, Harriet ran and hid in a pigpen. She stayed with the pigs for four days and nights, fighting them for potato scraps. Finally, she was so hungry that she went back to the house. When found, she was whipped twice: once for stealing the sugar and once for running away.

After a while, Harriet got better. But the injury had caused a problem. Harriet sometimes fell asleep suddenly—even if she was talking or working. Her master and overseers thought she was stupid. But they were wrong. Harriet noticed everything that went on around her. She noticed when slaves were whipped. She noticed when there wasn't enough food.

As Harriet grew older, she became angry that she was a slave. And she was angry that *anyone* could be a slave. She sometimes touched the deep scar on her forehead and thought of Jim running away. And she wondered, How would it feel to be free?

2 ESCAPE!

In 1844, Harriet married a man named John Tubman. John was a black man who had been born free. Harriet worked in the fields during the day and stayed with John in his cabin at night. She talked to him about running away, but he said she was foolish. He didn't understand why she would risk her life that way. Harriet decided to stay with John for the time being.

In 1849, something happened to change Harriet's mind. That year, her master died. Harriet heard that she and other slaves would be sold to a new master who lived farther south. As bad as it was to be a slave in Maryland, it was worse in the deep South. Life was much harsher on the cotton plantations there. Harriet knew what she had to do. She would run away after all, that very night. She didn't tell John. She didn't trust him to keep her secret.

Families were often broken up when slaves were sold to different masters. This illustration shows a mother being sold while her child is kept behind.

Desperate slaves tried many ways of escaping north.
This man mailed himself to the free city of Philadelphia
in a crate.

Harriet set out for freedom late at night.
Two of her brothers came with her, but
they soon became scared and wanted to go
back. They knew that if they were caught,
they would be punished severely. They
might even be killed. Harriet wanted to go
on without them, but they convinced her to
go back, too. At home again, she climbed
into bed with John. But she knew she
would try again.

Two nights later, Harriet wrapped a piece of bread in a cloth. Then she was on her way—this time alone. She knew of a kind white woman who might help her, and she found the woman's house. The woman gave Harriet two pieces of paper with names on them. They were the names of families who would help her on her way north. These slips of paper were Harriet's first "tickets" on the Underground Railroad.

The woman who helped Harriet may have been a Quaker, like the people pictured here. Quakers were opposed to slavery and believed that everyone was equal in the eyes of God.

Although the Underground Railroad was not really underground, some people did dig tunnels under their homes to hide runaways there.

The Underground Railroad was not a real railroad. And it was not underground. It was a group of people who helped runaway slaves. People in one house, or "station," might offer a place to hide and a meal to eat. Then they would show the runaway, or "passenger," how to get to the next station. Sometimes a person acted as a guide for runaways. These people were called "conductors."

Harriet traveled only at night, when it was easier to avoid being seen. She ran through fields and forests. She trudged through swamps and heavy brush. During the day, she hid in haystacks or fields. Sometimes she went to a station on the Underground Railroad, and people hid her in a barn, cellar, or attic.

Harriet headed north along the Choptank River into Delaware. On clear nights, she followed the shimmering North Star. On cloudy nights, she checked the trees. Her father had taught her that moss grows on the north side of trees.

Runaway slaves usually traveled at night through swamps and forests, where it was easy to hide.

The free city of Philadelphia during the 1850s

After many days of walking, Harriet finally made it to the northern city of Philadelphia, Pennsylvania. At last she was free! No one in the North could be made a slave. No overseers could whip her. No one could tell her what to do or how to do it. Harriet looked down at her hands to see if she was the same person. She felt like she was in heaven.

Philadelphia was a big city, with horses and wagons cramming the streets. People shouted at one another. Peddlers sold hats, apples, and cooking pots. Harriet found a job in a hotel kitchen. She was pleased to finally be paid for her work.

Philadelphia was also lonely. There was no one to welcome Harriet to the free land. But before long she met people who were part of the Underground Railroad. Soon, they made a plan for Harriet to rescue her sister's family. It would be very dangerous. Her master would have people looking for Harriet to return her to slavery. To Harriet, it was worth the risk.

William Still was a part of the Underground Railroad in Philadelphia. He later published a book about all the slaves he helped escape.

Harriet Tubman,
conductor on the
Underground Railroad

In December of 1850, Harriet returned to Maryland. Again, she hid during the day. She hurried through woods and swamps at night. Soon she was guiding her sister and her sister's two children back north to freedom. Harriet had become a conductor on the Underground Railroad.

A few months later, Harriet decided to make the dangerous trip south again. This time she rescued her brother and two other men. After that, she made many more trips south. Soon, Harriet became well known as a hero. Slaves whispered to one another about her bravery. They called her Moses. In the Bible, Moses rescued his people from slavery. Now Harriet Tubman was doing what she could to rescue hers.

"GO ON OR DIE"

Sometimes the people Harriet was rescuing became tired or scared. Sometimes they wanted to go back to their masters, or maybe just collapse where they were standing. Harriet knew that if any runaway gave up, Harriet and the other runaways would all be in danger. When a slave complained, Harriet pulled out a pistol she carried. "You'll go on or die," she said. After that, people always changed their minds. And Harriet always got them to freedom.

WANTED

J,OOO REWARD

3 A PRICE ON HER HEAD

In 1850, a new law made Harriet's work much harder. It was called the Fugitive Slave Law. It said that anyone who found runaway slaves had to report them so they could be returned to their master. Even a freed slave in the Northern states could be returned to slavery. Disobeying the law meant a big fine, and maybe jail.

Now Harriet had to bring slaves all the way to Canada. The journey to freedom was longer and more dangerous than ever. Authorities along the way worked harder to capture escaped slaves. Large rewards were offered for the capture of runaways.

But the Underground Railroad worked harder, too. Harriet became one of its best conductors. She had no fear of being caught—it was much more important to fight against slavery. Harriet said God would keep her safe.

Harriet (FAR LEFT, WITH PAN) and some former slaves she had rescued

CHICKEN RUN

On one rescue mission, Harriet had to pass through Bucktown, Maryland. One of her former masters still lived nearby. Harriet pulled her sun hat down over her face in case she ran into him. She also bought a couple live chickens. When she saw her former master coming toward her, she dropped the chickens. They squawked and fluttered, and Harriet scrambled on the ground trying to catch the screaming birds. Harriet's plan worked! The man didn't recognize her because he saw only the top of her hat. And he didn't suspect a thing.

By 1856, Harriet had rescued so many slaves that slave masters knew who she was. They offered a reward of $40,000 for her arrest. Still, Harriet kept on bringing slaves out of the South. She even rescued her parents, who could barely walk. She bought a home in Auburn, New York, to share with them.

Frederick Douglass was a fierce abolitionist and a good friend of Harriet.

Many people in the United States and Europe believed slavery was wrong, and they were working to end it. These people were called abolitionists. Harriet began to give speeches at abolitionist meetings across the country. She used the money she earned from these speeches to help rescue more slaves.

Once, on her way to a meeting in Boston, Harriet stopped in Troy, New York. There she heard that a runaway slave had been captured. He was in the courthouse and was going to be sent back to his owner. Harriet had to do something.

Quickly, she gathered a crowd of her abolitionist friends. She told some young boys to yell "Fire!" and the crowd grew even larger. When the authorities removed the slave from the courthouse, Harriet grabbed onto his arm. She knocked down two men and dragged the slave away. A huge fight broke out in the crowd, but Harriet carried the man through. Finally, she put him in a boat.

This image was published in a pamphlet by a group called the Anti-Slavery Society.

The slave escaped, but he was captured again on the other side of the river. Harriet didn't give up—she rescued him once more. This time, she successfully brought him to Canada.

Harriet's daring courthouse rescue was an important victory for abolitionists. People everywhere heard about Harriet's fight against slavery. When Harriet arrived in Boston, she spoke to crowds all over the city. More and more people agreed with Harriet that slavery was wrong. And she was more determined than ever to end it.

4 WAR HERO

In 1860, Abraham Lincoln was elected president of the United States. Lincoln believed slavery was wrong. Slave owners in the South worried that Lincoln would outlaw slavery. They said they could not run their farms and plantations without slaves.

After Lincoln was elected, seven Southern states decided to break off from the United States and form their own country. More Southern states soon joined them. Lincoln told the states that they could not break off from the United States. In April of 1861, the Southern army attacked a U.S. fort in South Carolina. The Civil War had begun.

With a war going on, Harriet's friends convinced her to stop traveling into the South to rescue slaves. Harriet agreed. She had made nineteen trips into the Southern states. She had rescued over three hundred people from slavery. It was time to look for new ways to help.

Abraham Lincoln led the United States through the Civil War.

During the Civil War, many black people in the South packed everything they had into wagons and fled to the North.

In the spring of 1862, the Union (Northern) Army freed many slaves in South Carolina. Despite the dangers of the war, Harriet went there to help the former slaves. These people had almost nothing. Harriet used the little money she had to build a laundry. That way, black women could earn money by washing clothes for the Union soldiers. Harriet showed other former slaves how to make items to sell to the soldiers.

Harriet worked for the Union Army in other ways. If the soldiers were hungry, she tied on an apron and cooked. If the army needed a nurse, she used roots and herbs to heal sick and wounded men. Harriet scrubbed floors, and she swatted flies. She served her country by doing whatever needed to be done.

Both free blacks and former slaves joined the Union Army to fight against the South.

Harriet even worked as a spy. Because of her time on the Underground Railroad, she knew her way through forests and across fields. And slaves in the South trusted her and shared information with her. She sneaked into Southern army camps and learned what she could about the army's plans.

BLACK SOLDIERS

About 200,000 black soldiers fought for the North during the Civil War. They were free blacks and escaped slaves. About 35,000 of them were killed in the fighting. Many whites believed that blacks would make poor soldiers. Some argued that blacks should not be allowed to serve. But black troops proved to be brave and valuable. Without black soldiers, the Union might not have won the war.

Harriet was a soldier, too. On the night of June 2, 1863, she helped lead about three hundred black Union soldiers up the Combahee River, near the coast of South Carolina. Harriet and the other soldiers removed bombs the Southerners had planted in the water. Then they sailed on huge gunboats upriver, near some plantations. The soldiers set fire to the plantations, sending the masters and overseers fleeing into the woods.

At first, the slaves on the burning plantations were frightened, but then they ran to the boats. Children screamed and hung on to their mothers' skirts. Harriet carried two pigs for a woman who was toting a child. As she ran, Harriet fell and tore her dress. But she kept hold of the pigs. When it was all over, about 750 slaves had been rescued. "Moses" was saving her people once again.

By the end of the war, many Southern cities— like Charleston, South Carolina—lay in ruins.

5 AFTER THE WAR

After four years of fighting, the North won the Civil War in April of 1865. And once and for all, slavery was against the law in every state. There would be no more need for the Underground Railroad. Harriet would never have to risk her life to free slaves again.

Harriet wanted to go back to her home in Auburn, New York, to be with her parents. As she boarded the train to go home, the conductor looked at her ticket. It was a half-price ticket. Anyone who fought in the war could ride for half the price. But the conductor told Harriet the train did not carry black people for half price.

This illustration from a newspaper shows members of the House of Representatives celebrating after the Thirteenth Amendment was passed. This law made slavery illegal in every state.

Harriet refused to get off the train, and the man grabbed her arm. He quickly discovered that Harriet was stronger than he was, so he called three other men to help. The four men twisted her arm and shoved her into a baggage car.

Harriet rode in the baggage car all the way home. She was uncomfortable, and her arm was badly hurt. But something else hurt even worse. Slavery was now against the law, but black people were still a long way from being treated equally.

This photo of Harriet was taken during the 1860s.

Some black Americans, like these laborers, found paying jobs after the war. But many had a hard time finding work and feeding their families.

At last, Harriet arrived at home. She enjoyed catching up with her parents and friends. She could rest knowing that no one had to worry about being caught and sent back into slavery.

Harriet was still famous, and she received many visitors. Most were former slaves who were poor and sick. They asked for food, clothes, and medicine. Harriet had almost no money, but she did what she could to help.

Harriet was friends with Susan B. Anthony, an important leader in the fight for women's rights.

The government had refused to pay Harriet for her work during the war. So Harriet worked at whatever jobs she could find. She also raised chickens and grew a vegetable garden. Door to door, Harriet sold the chickens and vegetables. She also earned money by giving speeches. She spoke about fair treatment for black people and women.

In this way, Harriet managed to support herself and her parents, and to help anyone who came to her door. She even opened two schools so children of former slaves could learn to read and write.

In 1869, Harriet married a former slave named Nelson Davis. She had met Nelson at an army base in South Carolina.

PLANTING APPLES

When Harriet was a young slave, her master did not let her eat any apples from the trees he forced her to plant. The little girl decided that when she got older, she would grow apples—not for herself, but for *other* people to eat. Many years later, when Harriet was an old woman, she remembered her plan. Though she hadn't planted apple trees, she said she had still carried out her plan. All the things she had done for other people, like helping slaves to freedom and caring for the needy, were like planting apples for other people to eat.

Harriet near the end of her life

Nelson died in 1888. Because he had been in the army, Harriet finally received some money from the government. She saved the $20 a month the government gave her. After eight years, she had enough money to buy the land across the street from her house. She opened a home for sick and needy African Americans. In 1911, when Harriet was about ninety-one years old, she moved in there herself.

Harriet was happy in the home. She had many visitors, and she loved to tell stories—especially about the Underground Railroad. On the evening of March 10, 1913, Harriet gathered several friends at her bed. She had pneumonia, and she knew she was going to die soon.

Although Harriet was sick, she was not too weak to sing. She asked her friends to sing with her. As Harriet Tubman lay dying, their voices filled her room.

The Harriet Tubman Home in Auburn, New York

TIMELINE

In the year . . .

1826   Harriet was put to work checking muskrat traps.   Age 6

1830   she was working as hard as a man in the fields.

1835   she was hit in the head with an iron weight after refusing to stop a runaway slave.   Age 15

1844   she married John Tubman.

1849   she escaped from slavery.

1850   she went back into the South to rescue her sister and her sister's family.
the Fugitive Slave Law was passed.   Age 30

1857   she rescued her parents.

1860   she saved a captured slave from a courthouse in Troy, New York.

1861   the Civil War began on April 12.

1862   she traveled to South Carolina to help newly freed slaves.

1863   she led 300 troops up the Combahee River and freed about 750 slaves.   Age 43

1865   the Civil War ended.
she was attacked and thrown in a baggage car by a train conductor and three other men.

1869   she married Nelson Davis.

1888   Nelson Davis died.

1896   she bought the twenty-five acres of land across the road from her house to build a home for the sick and needy.   Age 76

1913   she died of pneumonia on March 10.   Age 93

REMEMBERING HARRIET TUBMAN

Many people honored Harriet for her bravery when she was alive. Queen Victoria of England awarded her a silver medal and invited her to England to celebrate the queen's birthday. Even more honors came to Harriet after she died. A ship was named after her. A park in Auburn, New York, was built in her honor. And in 1995, the United States issued a postage stamp showing Harriet leading slaves to freedom. In Auburn, New York, the Harriet Tubman Home is a museum. It stands as a tribute to her life and her work.

FURTHER READING

NONFICTION

Bial, Raymond. *The Underground Railroad.* **Boston: Houghton Mifflin Company, 1995.** Gives a history of the Underground Railroad and includes many photos.

Ferris, Jeri. *Go Free or Die: A Story about Harriet Tubman.* **Minneapolis, MN: Carolrhoda Books, Inc., 1993.** Tells the dramatic story of Harriet's escape from slavery. Includes illustrations.

Sullivan, George. *Harriet Tubman.* **New York: Scholastic, 2001.** Tells the story of Harriet Tubman's life, using interviews with Harriet as well as the words of her friends.

Weidt, Maryann N. *Voice of Freedom: A Story about Frederick Douglass.* **Minneapolis, MN: Carolrhoda Books, Inc., 2001.** Tells the story of Frederick Douglass, who was born a slave but escaped at age twenty and worked tirelessly for the antislavery cause. Douglass and Harriet Tubman were good friends.

FICTION

Petry, Ann. *Harriet Tubman: Conductor on the Underground Railroad.* **New York: Harper Trophy, 1996.** The classic, novel-length, fictionalized story of Harriet's life.

Rappaport, Doreen. *Freedom River.* **New York: Jump at the Sun, 2000.** A picture book for older readers. Tells the story of John Parker, an ex-slave who becomes a successful businessman and an active conductor on the Underground Railroad.

WEBSITES

Aboard the Underground Railroad
<http://www.cr.nps.gov/nr/travel/underground/>
Supported by the National Park Service, this website
provides descriptions and photographs of fifty-five historic
places that were associated with the Underground Railroad.
It also includes a history of slavery and a map of the most
common escape routes taken on the Underground Railroad.

The Harriet Tubman Home
<http://www.nyhistory.com/harriettubman/index.htm>
The website for the Harriet Tubman Home, where Harriet
died, which still stands in Auburn, New York. The website
gives Harriet's story, a history of the home, photos, and tour
information.

SELECT BIBLIOGRAPHY

Bradford, Sarah. *Harriet Tubman: The Moses of Her People.*
1886. Reprint, Bedford, MA: Applewood Books, 1993.

Bradford, Sarah. *Scenes in the Life of Harriet Tubman.*
1869. Reprint, Salem, NH: Ayer Company, Publishers,
Inc., 1992.

Conrad, Earl. *Harriet Tubman.* New York: International
Publishers, 1942.

Conrad, Earl. *Harriet Tubman.* Washington, D.C.: The
Associated Publishers, Inc., 1943.

Gorrel, Gena K. *North Star to Freedom: The Story of the
Underground Railroad.* New York: Delacorte Press, 1996.

INDEX

Acknowledgements

For photographs: © Schomburg Center for Research in Black Culture, pp. 4, 42; Georgia Historical Society, p. 7; © North Wind Picture Archives, pp. 8, 14, 16, 18, 19, 20; National Archives, pp. 9, 33, 39; Courtesy of the North Carolina Division of Archives and History, p. 10; Library of Congress, pp. 15, 21, 30, 31, 35, 37, 38; Ohio Historical Society, p. 17; © Sophia Smith Collection/Smith College, p. 24; *Dictionary of American Portraits*, pp. 26, 40; Delaware Public Archives, p. 27; © Leib Image Archives, p. 32; © Lee Snider/CORBIS, p. 43; © U.S. Postal Service, p. 45. Front cover: Library of Congress (photo); Corbis Royalty Free Images (frame). Back cover: © Jim Simondet/Independent Picture Service.

For quoted material: p. 22, Conrad, Earl. *Harriet Tubman.* New York: International Publishers, 1942.